Excuses, excuses

What 'reason' do you use when you fly off the handle?

Did someone else say something, do something or forget to do something? Maybe you got into an argument and the other person wouldn't listen. Did a family member or a neighbour make too much noise? Was it your child, brother, sister or friend that pushed your buttons?

Whatever your excuse, and however much you feel like lashing out at the time, the truth is, getting angry gets you nowhere.

Except into trouble, into hospital, and out of relationships. Lose your temper all the time and you'll probably lose everything, eventually.

And anyway, temper tantrums are for kids.

They're what you do when you lose it. When all you can think of is throwing your toys out of the pram. When you don't know the difference between being strong and being aggressive.

Know what we think?

IT'S WEAK TO STAY AND ARGUE

Doesn't sound right, does it?

A lot of people say that standing your ground is strong, that you should look up to people who don't take any nonsense.

But think about it. What happens when you lose your temper? Things get out of control and you get into trouble. People steer clear of you. You end up on your own.

What's so strong about that?

Wouldn't it be better NOT to shout and lash out? Wouldn't it be better to be admired for being calm and in control?

This book can help you do that, but you'll have to be strong. A lot stronger than your angry self.

Strong stuff next

IT'S STRONG TO KEEP YOUR COOL

Get a different plan

Strong, calm, controlled people choose to avoid aggravation in the first place, or they choose to react differently when they feel their hackles start to rise.

It takes real strength to do this. It's much easier to lose it, shout or swear, stamp your feet or throw a punch.

But this book will help you take the tougher option. When you use the 3-step plan that comes later, you'll really get to know your own temper and how to keep it under control.

You'll become calmer, quieter, more powerful. And the people who count will know that you're a much stronger person than you used to be.

YOU GOT A PROBLEM WITH THAT?

It's not strong to lose it

If you still think losing control of yourself isn't stupid, think about this:

Imagine you're driving a fast car and you come to a tight bend with a slippery surface. You're going to need all your skill to stay on the road, so you take a deep breath, remember everything you've learned about driving, grip the wheel and control the car until the danger is past.

What would happen if you lost it, instead? If you let a red mist come down and you got angry at the bend because it was too tight? You'd skid, wouldn't you? You, the car and your passengers would end up in the ditch, in the hospital or in the graveyard.

In your life, you're always in that car. Your aim is to finish your journey in one piece. That slippery bend is just something that 'pushes your buttons'.

Lost it!

Use your skill to stay in control. Lose your temper and you don't.

Now ask what's in it for you

WHAT'S IN IT FOR ME?

Big respect

The self-respect you earn when you stay in control and use your skill and strength to handle a tough situation.

The respect of your friends and family who look at you in a new way and start to realise that you're stronger than they thought.

The respect of strangers who, when you speak calmly or walk away from angry situations, know that you helped to make things better, not worse.

There's not much that's more important than making good decisions. If you agree, and think you're strong enough to try our 3-step plan, turn the page and…

Let's get started!

IT'S EASY TO BE STRONG

As easy as...

Know your buttons

Think about what makes you angry. The people or places that always seem to get you going. When you know your buttons, you can keep them from being pressed.

Know your early warning system

You feel different just before you snap. With some people it's heavy breathing. Others feel the blood pounding in their ears. Learn to spot these signs so you can move to step 3 before they turn into trouble.

Know where the escape hatches are

You just decide to react differently this time. Some people pause and count to 10, or decide to walk away. Others have calming words that they say, that de-fuse a situation. When you have a few of these up your sleeve, you'll be able to stay in control whatever happens.

Breathe!

As soon as you've responded differently, give yourself respect. You're strong. You're in control. You've steered the car round that slippery corner without losing it.

You've been strong enough to keep your temper.

So let's do it

KNOW
YOUR
BUTTONS

What always gets you going?

Something someone says at home? What about your friends? Other people? What about when people are noisy around you or tell you what to do?

Is it your brother/sister, a boss, the government, the police, traffic wardens, white vans? Do you suffer from road rage? (Actually, you don't, it's everybody around you that suffers).

What about when you drink? Is it worse then? And when you're having a night out, does just being with your friends make you feel like arguing or fighting?

These are all buttons. You need to think about them so that you know exactly which ones apply to you. Then you need to write them down on the next 2 pages.

Why? Because when you know your buttons, you can keep them from being pressed. Go to different places. Spend time with different friends. Ignore other people's comments. Get control of the car, steer round the corner and forget about what other drivers are doing.

FEELING LEFT OUT

BEING TOLD OFF

BEING IGNORED

This way to the buttons

My Buttons

Write down the things that make you lose your temper or get irritable

What gets me going?

What gets me going?

Step 2 next

KNOW YOUR EARLY WARNING SYSTEM

Feeling tense?

Think about the last time you lost your temper. How did you feel just beforehand? Can you remember what happened, physically or mentally?

You may have started breathing heavily, clenched your fists, stood up suddenly, folded your arms, drummed on the table with your fingers. Some people really do see a red mist in front of their eyes.

Or maybe your early warnings are in your mind. You start to feel critical of someone else. You don't think much of their appearance, their voice, their clothes, their opinions. Maybe you feel ignored or think people are looking down on you.

All these signs are really useful, because they warn you that you're getting near to losing it. They're like a road sign that says 'Slippery corner ahead'.

Think about the signs that apply to you and write down as many as you can on the next two pages.

List this way

My Early Warning System

Write down all the things you think and feel,
just before you lose it

Feeling hot or breathing hard (for example)

USE THE ESCAPE HATCH

This is when you react differently

Here's when you count to 10, or change the subject, or walk away, or sit down, relax your shoulders and breathe deeply.

Some people 'switch on' some music in their head when they get one of their early warning signs.

Others have a few words that they whisper to take the heat out of the situation ('slippery corner, watch the road ahead' are good ones).

You need to have a choice of escape hatches and be ready to use one whenever you get an early warning sign.

You can invent your own, of course, that fit with the buttons you wrote down earlier. Or you can turn the page and see some of the escape hatches that other people use. They won't mind you borrowing them.

More ideas this way

MORE ESCAPE HATCHES

Walk away

Here's a great solution. If you can, make an excuse and leave before things escalate. You don't need to agree or back down, but choose to leave - maybe saying "Can we talk about this later".

Say "You might be right about that"

This works best when you really disagree with someone. Instead of arguing and getting angry, just say "You might be right about that". You don't have to mean it, it's an escape hatch. Often, the other person will be so surprised that all the tension will drain away. An alternative is to say "I understand what you mean/respect your opinion ... but..".

Sit down

When we're about to explode, we need to be standing, so we can fight, or run, or seem bigger than we are.

It's a lot harder to get into trouble when you're sitting down though, so when you get an early warning, stay in your seat, or go find one.

Hum

We're serious. What's your favourite song? Get into the habit of quietly or even silently humming it to yourself when you get an early warning. Use it to change your focus. It works even better with slow, calming tunes.

And finally

BREATHE

Relax your shoulders and breathe slowly

Often, your shoulders are up around your ears when tension builds. If you notice this in time and make a point of relaxing and letting them drop, you'll calm yourself and others too. Breathe slowly and think about those slippery corners while you do it.

When you breathe, close your mouth – it's hard to over-breathe through your nose.

And as you breathe, reconnect with your body and surroundings. Use it to centre yourself – to step back and notice your reactions.

Stop, think and reflect.

Use the breaths to focus and change how you react.

Feels great doesn't it?

SO
NEXT
TIME

Follow the plan

Know your buttons

Get to know the buttons on your list. When you know them, you can keep them from being pressed.

Know your early warning system

Learn your danger signs and look out for them so that you can move to step 3 before they turn into trouble.

Know where the escape hatches are

React differently. Count to 10, walk away, say the phrase, hum the tune. Whatever your chosen escapes are, use one as soon as you get an early warning sign.

Breathe!

Now give yourself respect.

You're powerful. You're in control. You've steered the car round that slippery corner without losing it.

You're strong enough to keep your temper!
Now, time to make a plan. Pick one small thing to practice or change. Then use the Planner sheet on pages 30/31 to give yourself the best start.

Once you're done, use the Review sheet on pages 32/33 to check your progress.

Go, make a plan

Planner Sheet

Make a Plan!

1. What am I going to do?

Just one small thing

2. When am I going to do it?

That way you'll know if you don't do it

3. What problems or difficulties could arise, and how can I overcome them?

4. Is my planned task -

	Yes	No
• Useful for understanding or changing how I am?		
• Specific, so that I will know when I have done it?		
• Realistic, practical and achievable?		

My notes:

living
life to
the full
www.llttf.com

Review Sheet

How did it go? What did you plan to do?

If yes: What went well?

What didn't go so well?

What have you learned from what happened?

How are you going to apply what you have learned?

From the:
Living life to the full
resources.

Download from

www.llttf.com/resources

Did you try to do it?

Yes   No

If no: What stopped you?

External things (other people, work or home issues etc.)

Internal things (forgot, not enough time, put it off, didn't think I could do it, couldn't see the point etc.)

How can you tackle things differently next time?

WHERE TO GET EVEN MORE ADVICE AND SUPPORT

The 1,2,3 Breathe method is a great way to stay in control. If you're wanting more information about our approach, click on **www.llttf.com.**

It's free and the number one site for low mood and anxiety recommended by NHS Trusts and teams in England.* It's packed with ways to lift your mood and start living a happier and healthier life.

Go for it!

*Bennion et al, 2017. BMJ Open http://bmjopen.bmj.com/content/7/1/e014844